XXOO

"IT'S ALL ABOUT STYLE"

The Well-Traveled Home

SANDRA ESPINET
The Well-Traveled Home

GIBBS SMITH
TO ENRICH AND INSPIRE HUMANKIND

I dedicate this book to every airplane that has taken me

far and away and opened my eyes to the world.

Peace through design and love through fabulosity.

CONTENTS

INTRODUCTION

First, a confession: I didn't come to the life of a transcontinental nomad overnight, or easily or even on purpose. As a child, I was essentially in tow to busy parents as my father practiced his profession across time zones. So, of necessity, I turned the 737s of Avianca and VIASA and TWA into my homes away from home. Everything—from the newspapers and magazines left behind in the seat pockets to the duty-free gift shops of international terminals—informed my young understanding of what I thought was attractive and worthy and exciting in the world. In other words, I simply did what any other bewildered kid does when dragged along on the agenda set by her parents: I made the most of the situation. I watched and learned and took notes and hoped that the future would afford me the opportunity to integrate all of my impressions into something cohesive—a look, an outfit, a group of friends, a suite of furniture, a seaside villa of many rooms. A passion.

You know, when unique objects and found treasures from anyone's travels are pulled together, they tell an authentic and personal story. As an interior designer, the compelling challenge for me, then, is to ensure that this story is beautiful and accessible to my clientele and their families and friends going forward, that this story is as visually arresting and appealing as it is welcoming and comfortable. I suppose I would say that the essence of my interior design work seeks to reflect the evolving interplay of the domestic and the international, while remaining true to my intent to create alluring family living spaces and home environments.

Blending the fabulous objects culled from particular corners of the globe is a delicate art form. Over the years, I have endeavored to fearlessly embrace the space between our conventional notions of here and there, of home and away, and to make that uncertain terrain my playground, atelier and design forte. As *The Well-Traveled Home* will illustrate, the outcomes possible in this territory can and should be spectacular—a crossroads between ideas and space, wood and steel, wet and dry, al fresco and enclosure, Frieda Kahlo and Velasquez, you and me.

I describe my role in this process as a mix-master of eclectic convergence, a specialist in the fearless melding of exotic elements with traditional furnishings from our neck of the woods into stylish and unforgettable presentations of comfort and calm, exhilaration and extravagance—in a word, the world. In truth, fitting the right pieces into the right rooms within a plausible design scheme is my ultimate happiness. It is how I process and make sense of the data dump world we all must wade through.

Professionally, I have been navigating this shape-shifting line between the sublime look of the lobbies of the Four Seasons in New York or the Danieli in Venice or the jewel-like riads of Tangier and the fun but misfortunate kitsch of tiki and tapas bars, import/export emporiums, and revival-this and homage-that for the better part of the last decade and change, all across the Americas, in flip-flops with a beat-up Birkin bag. I have accumulated a discerning though exuberant clientele who are *au fait* with transcontinental hopscotching across the United States as well as Europe, Asia, northern Africa, and both coasts of Latin America. My clients appreciate the spoils resulting from my personal appetite for adventure to the remotest outposts of the least likely countries. I have championed for them a sort of post-expedition take on the incorporation of the exotic and the banal—fewer zebra stripes and Chinatown lanterns, more Moroccan ceramics and Turkish metal sconces and pendants. I have sought out the new, the vibrant, and the authentic from far-flung cultures and occasionally inhospitable marketplaces with quality, design integrity, and "beautiful usefulness" as the watchwords of ultimate importance.

As a lifelong gypsy, I subject each and every acquisition to my own contrived litmus test: Will I begrudgingly maintain this bureau or will I cherish it from now onward, moving it with care and judging it worth the freight? The nonessential reveals itself pretty quickly using this strict guideline. My mantra is obviously "go big," but going big can be executed in reverse, by removal or restraint. Not every corner or every wall will need to be occupied with adornment. The resulting sparer, barer aesthetic in my work features a lot of uncovered stone and tile floors and naked masonry or plastered walls so that the importance of harmonized furniture and lighting and accessories is crucial and dramatic.

These interiors are meant to soothe and inspire; there isn't time or tendency for overly ornate spaces cluttered with opulent antiques. I've read myself quoted and I naturally agree that I will always prefer "a simple view of the ocean to a fussy rococo seventeenth-century desk." The design elements that have come to represent my signature style elegantly corroborate this point of view: the sweeping al fresco orientation of rooms featuring magnificent vistas, bold and elemental furnishings, exquisitely wrought artisanal pieces, dramatic artworks and exotic accessories sourced from all over the world. This nomadic work process and the thinking behind the correct blending of assorted possessions and acquisitions

of the well-traveled client, the artful combination of the contemporary with the antique, the repurposing of various native architectural elements, the interplay of the cosmopolitan with the rustic is now second nature to me.

Surprisingly, I am a native of the tiny Caribbean nation of Trinidad and Tobago, but my actual upbringing, education and evolving career in the design world have had me traveling the length and breadth of the Americas again and again. As the daughter of a petroleum supervisor, I moved with my family every few years "following the oil," from western Canada to the Altiplano of Bolivia and Peru to the Orinoco Oil Belt of Venezuela. I quickly developed a talent for making each new address feel if not entirely familiar then at least comfortable and home-like. Over the years my attraction to the vibrant color palette of the Andean indigenous peoples melded seamlessly with my love of the golden and emerald richness of the coastal pre-Columbians of northern South America. It was always the "tasteful" interiors shown on American television or in American magazines that seemed exotic to me in my youth, although I did come to appreciate New England restraint after attending college in Boston—all of that rectilinear order and puritanical symmetry.

Oddly, this unorthodox background, the tropics,

New England, and Los Angeles laid the groundwork for what now feels to me like a sixth sense with artful blending of the decorative arts from many quite different cultures. Middle Eastern inlaid bone chests, Thai carvings, Moroccan pottery and Mexican travertine never seemed unlikely décor companions to me. As will be seen across the pages of *The Well Traveled Home*, my pretty extensive body of residential and resort work is really a celebration of global culture and décor, arrangements of artistic traditions that are allowed to speak and serve in harmony with each other. The beautiful photography of my close collaborator, Hector Velazco, continues to thrill and motivate me and refresh my own taste and incite my desire for further and farther travels.

My ultimate point is that design solutions know no nationality. Well-traveled homes are living theaters that invite collaboration on a daily basis from any and all inhabitants—beloved families, old friends, new guests . . . and unexpected treasures.

TRAVEL & DESIGN

That descriptive phrase *well traveled*, often attached to international diplomats, film stars, CEOs and artists, is actually really hard to define. For many it simply means extensive exposure to countries ringing the globe, an offhand familiarity with the time difference between Sydney and Los Angeles, the likelihood of finding a nice piece of worked gold in Mexico's Taxco de Alarcon (not at all likely) or silk brocade in India's Banaras (a no-brainer). Probably *well traveled* implies a casual ability to pleasantly negotiate oneself in a variety of languages with some semblance of humor and a knack for knowing not just what to wear but what definitely what *not* to wear out for drinks in that silk road hotspot Istanbul. After a certain amount of observation and a smattering of history in a distant land, anyone will find oneself with an acquired taste for local cuisine and a working knowledge of indigenous art and décor. These are the advantages and perhaps even the obligations of those of us fortunate enough to travel for work or pleasure or both.

But sometimes the takeaway from even a casual brush with someone similarly well traveled can be superficial and perfunctory—a rather "been there, done that" sort of apathy or disinterest that has always left me disap-

pointed, feeling shortchanged. That whole Eurocentric worldview is just not my bag, not openhearted, not sincere. I mean, look at this passport: what else have you got to say about a month meandering from Cairo to Cape Town? Perhaps because the dislocating travel in my own childhood was mandatory, I never experience any new culture from the safety of the knowledge that I am just a plane ride away from home, as my round-trip ticket indicates. I was always taught to get comfortable in my new surroundings and craft them into a new and do-able conception of home for however long I might be in residence. It's an entirely different set of marching orders with which to decorate the structure that will shelter a life for an indeterminate length of time.

So with due credit to that old saying "necessity is the mother of invention," I took note of the homegrown solutions to design challenges that my Peruvian or Albertan next-door neighbors had perfected and had no qualms about adopting them into my own personal laundry list of design options. I will say that, even today, while I definitely have preferences for segments of the color wheel and spatial arrangement of sitting areas and window treatments, I am fundamentally open to every

last option from any corner of the globe to achieve what anyone wants in an interior: cleanliness, inspiration, function and beauty. I am wholeheartedly in favor of incorporating elemental design solutions from beyond the traditional Western canon altogether. I love asymmetry and a size disparity among furnishings and uneven areas of richness and sparseness. When I hear myself described as "well traveled" (or describe myself that way), what I think that really means is that I am eager and willing to lean into a variety of alien design aesthetics and believe that something that works in Peru can be paired with something that works in Dallas or Tangier and so on. In my experience, the sum is usually more vivid and iconoclastic and, importantly, successful than the alternative of irreproachable good taste.

As far as how my own life of travel continues to enhance and influence my design work, it is analogous to my South American passion for big-arena boxing: an excellent defense will only prevent you from losing the bout; it's the offense that leaves its mark with the judges and will make any hope of winning possible.

The entry hall is a home's first opportunity to convey a sense of personality and power of place. The historic Spanish Colonial style is the inspiration here. An old church bench, antique olive jars from Spain, a mirror found in San Miguel de Allende, and traditional ironwork perfects the impression. The style continues from a guest room all the way down to the wood carving of a custom-made doorknob.

Upholstered furnishings and an array of global decor mix together for a relaxed, sumptuous living room. The palette was inspired by the colors of the view—sand and sky. Guatemalan textile pillows and an Elizabeth Eakins cotton rug perk up the space with prints and pattern. A traditional Moroccan panel adds unexpected visual interest.

A bold and arresting portrait of an Indian youth by Mexican artist David Villasenor hangs over a Spanish desk illuminated by a lamp fashioned from an antique Provençal pottery jar. A simple color scheme of strong earth tones creates a vibrant, inviting atmosphere and offers a visual punch without relying on layers of pattern or objects.

River rock–inlaid headboards custom built into the wall imbue this elevated bedroom with indigenous energy. A painting of a Mexican village by ex-pat artist Dennis Wentworth Porter unifies the use of bold colors and patterns on the bedding. Exposed beams and unadorned wooden Mexican trunks on iron stands enhance the authentic mood with a rustic edge.

Deep melon walls are bold and arresting, the perfect choice for this dramatic master bath. Custom-made Moroccan shutters, a pair of mirrors with Chinese motif frames, and pillowed travertine tiles create an environment that is opulent but not overwhelming. An Indonesian wood sculpture provides an exotic accent.

Beautiful yet practical handcrafted tabletop items by skilled artisans from around the world, each noteworthy for distinctive design, form an exquisite collection.

My love of open-air living, white interiors, and an overall vibe of casual elegance is evident in these dining scenarios. For a covered terrace, I worked closely with local artisans to re-create a tile table from a historical design. In the classically styled dining room, a built-in cabinet of Moorish design frames a painting of a Mexican dancer. A magnificent wrought-iron chandelier with hand-blown amber glass balances the large room without dominating it.

My signature medley of pattern, fabrics, and worldly flair unite these guest rooms. In one, an antique door converted into a headboard works with a more neutral palette and creates a soothing sanctuary. In the other, a palette of cool, clean blues takes its cue from the spectacular view. A French rococo mirror articulates the space above the upholstered headboard. Fortuny fabric pillows punctuate both bed-scapes.

Subdued palette, uncluttered lines, and high ceilings create an airy ambience in a home office space. Artwork by Canadian painter Sondra Richardson and a Nepalese rug supply pattern and subtle doses of color. Contemporary woodcarvings from India, ammonite fossil shell from the Sahara, and blue coral from the Caribbean provide decorative artifacts. A Venetian glass Donghia lamp with an elegant silhouette and a tufted upholstered headboard collaborate beautifully in a small guest room.

A fearless use of color, juxtaposition of prints, and bold patterns animate this vibrant bedroom. An elaborately ornate Indian rug and hand-painted bedstead add unexpected whimsy. A substantial Mexican armoire and side tables bring it all down to earth. The twisted iron curtain rods are custom made.

Originally used to store and export olive oil from Spain, small earthenware jars purchased in Cairo are cradled in vintage holders and mounted over an Indonesian bench. Pillows are fashioned from vintage Guatemalan textiles and Afghan rugs. Similarly, old and new fabrics in a lively jumble work together in a bedroom. The upholstered iron bed frame is by a Mexican artisan.

Gorgeous in blue, this bedroom features
an elaborately turned four-poster bed and
an abundance of vividly patterned pillows,
bedding, and textiles. A bright cotton rug
keeps the exciting attitude going underfoot.

A small kilim rug, an antique mirror from San Miguel de Allende, blue Talavera tile from Puebla, and an ornate chandelier found in Guadalajara bring the bygone glamour of Spanish Colonial culture into the modern-day home. Travertine floors and slab counter finish the look. Moorish and European influences are prevalent in the entryway, where an aesthetic medley of antique Moroccan lanterns, a mosaic floor, and an old Spanish church bench welcome the visitor with a touch of elegance and unique character.

The restrained palette of a paneled bedroom delivers high style and collaborates with the masculine mood of the architecture. A master suite tableau is elegantly appointed with an eclectic grouping of antique furnishings, contemporary fabrics, and decorative accents from India, Europe, and Africa.

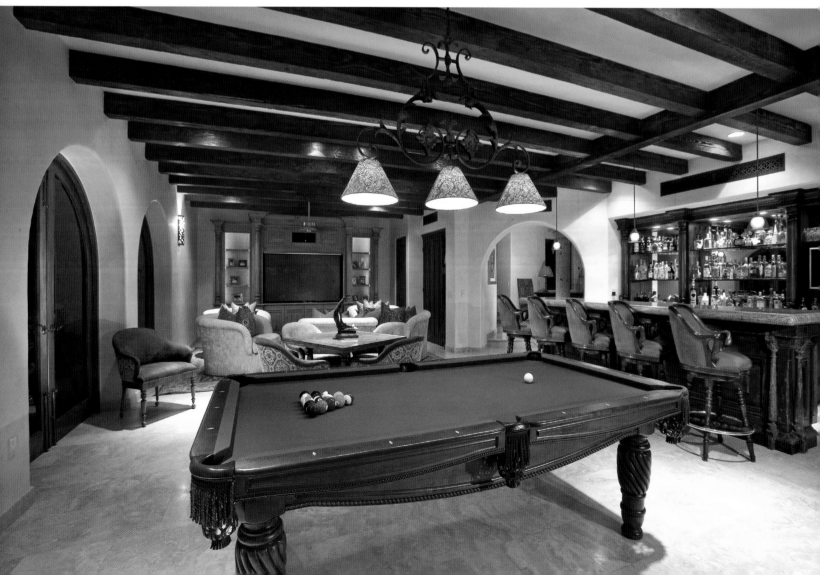

The view is the star of a living room, which features an old Indian door converted into a coffee table and Moroccan lanterns fashioned into a chandelier. In the game room, an old Guatemalan pharmaceutical counter has been repurposed as a bar. Above, an elaborately carved Thai panel becomes a gorgeous focal point over a traditional *cantera*, or console table, for the wall of a covered terrace. Vietnamese planters, artisanal sconces, and modern sculptural hurricane lamps lend stylistic layers.

A vintage Indonesian daybed and ornate, octagonal Moroccan table hold court in a ravishing and relaxing outdoor terrace rich with classical elegance.

ADVENTURE & ARTIFACT

Conventional wisdom in the design world holds that accessories can make or break an interior—and it's true. Personal possessions and ornaments imbue a living space with the client's character and history, and arranging these final flourishes has always been as creatively rewarding to me as the initial grand conception.

But it's also true that in today's easily traveled world, the alien and exotic are no farther away than our laptops or a quick trip to the designer district in the nearest metro area, where smart shops stuffed with containers full of pre-edited fabrics, furnishings, and fixtures from buying trips through the Andes, Asia, or the flea markets of European capitals are as ubiquitous these days as Moroccan poufs. Unfortunately, the incredible convenience of online bazaars has also served to slightly divorce the acquisition and display of exotic artifacts from any organic evolution or personal relevance to the client or designer—which is why my approach swerves sharply from this keyboard-clicking, à la carte, retail route.

Call me literal, I still love to explore in the field, as it were, and discover overlooked relics washed up on

foreign shores or beautiful handcrafted work still being created by native artisans.

Which reminds me of a story of almost slapstick dimensions that makes less intrepid designers in their skinny wrap dresses gasp in mock amazement. A few years ago, my husband and I went with a group of good friends on photographic safari in northern India searching for the elusive and sadly diminishing Bengal tiger. Rajasthan was a part of India that was less known to me then and held great appeal. We had seen phenomenal wildlife from the backs of our Jeeps for five days when I decided to remain in camp one day and stop bouncing. Within a few hours I was bored and anxious to take flight but soon discovered that all the Jeeps were gone. Never one to sit idly by and await rescue, I cajoled one of the guides with our party to saddle up (if that is the correct term) two of the henna-painted camels so we could do a little sightseeing. My persuasiveness was rewarded after a two-hour hump to the nearest village, when my guide and I stumbled upon what turned out to be a women's collective of traditional textile artists! The unexpected tableau was breathtaking—a kaleidoscopic blur of crim-

sons, magentas, indigos and violets, piled into heaps of handcrafted fabric. I dropped down off of my camel and with my guide translating asked dozens of questions about the dyes, the weaves, the symbols, the time it took, the intended users, etc., and was rewarded with enthusiastic answers, aesthetic disclosures, and passionate perceptions. These women had little expectation of finding purchasers for their gorgeous textiles and much less of encountering an interior designer from the West looking to reward their efforts and personal stories with a gracious purchase of the whole lot, but that is exactly what I did!

Technically, cherished weavings such as these are not impossible to acquire in Los Angeles or Miami or from a Delhi-based exporter, and I am all for the free exchange of goods and services. But it delighted me to offer my clients these textiles and to impress upon them the context of their creation. It might be a small matter or even an outdated point of honor to expect some respect in the marketplace for the expertise and emotions of the creators, but in my work and in my view, it makes all the difference.

Consequently, I have converted many a stray week in the Middle East or rained-out Caribbean vacation or family voyage in Asia into an investigation of what is out there, or as my husband calls it, a "National Geographic shopping adventure." Incorporating my discoveries of precious artifacts into delightful, inspired and organic decor for my clientele is what I live for. I am happy to do the legwork; in fact, I prefer it. Don't get me wrong. I frequently find myself clicking "Buy Now" and completing the formalities with the credit card. In less than a week the object in question arrives, but the transaction always feels anti-climactic somehow. Great. I got it. No need to make life unnecessarily complicated or arduous, but make it too easy all the time and my theory is why bother. Perhaps the journey really is the point, really is the finish line. I think so.

The spirit of the Mexican hacienda is positively alive in this spacious living area overlooking the Sea of Cortez. Modern shapes and finishes eloquently mingle with traditional architectural motifs to create a powerful sense of mood and place.

A spice-tone palette becomes the custom umbrella and lounge chair cushions on an outdoor terrace surrounding a pool. In the living room vignette above, earthy hues unify modern fabrics and vintage Indonesian textiles. A beautifully carved antique Guatemalan table adds uncommon visual interest.

A unique layered architectural style marries modern opulence with solid, classical sensibility in a powder room. The variegated chocolate travertine cut in rectilinear form provides an exciting contrast with the detail of an extravagantly carved Indian mirror. An old Guatemalan cabinet, Moroccan urns striped with metallic paint, Coptic crosses, and a fabulous ecclesiastical scene achieve perfect balance in a dynamic entry foyer.

The vibrant and energizing palette of this fun and unpretentious bedroom is inspired by the stylistic traditions of San Miguel de Allende. Visually striking but eminently comfortable, the furnishings deliver the patina of history and sweeten the sense of escape.

Spanish Colonial sconces from San Miguel de Allende flank a stunning antique mirror above a console accessorized with antique altarpieces. In a small bedroom, a headboard upholstered in plain ivory leather stands up to the room's bold palette of burnt terra-cotta. An Ethiopian Coptic cross decorates the Tibetan bedside chest. Each bed in a kids' room has its own niche; a bamboo blade fan adds a touch of the tropics.

Fortuny fabric and gorgeous nightstands by Formations create a spirited, ornamental master bedroom environment. In a little girls' room, antique Indian carousel horses mounted over beds throw the space into a delightful, whimsical direction. Above, a headboard with a Moroccan donkey arch silhouette is upholstered with an intricate Donghia fabric. An African shell basket and an old Chinese cabinet keep in sync with the home's handcrafted features.

A mélange of antique furnishings from Spain, Guatemala, and India make a warm and vibrant dining area conducive to convivial entertaining. Above, dark coral Venetian plasterwork serves as the backdrop for an elegant powder room, which mingles an ornate French mirror with a sleek Deco vanity for an artfully stunning result.

The style benefits of relaxed living by the ocean are on full display in this bright teal blue bedroom. The spacious master suite provides a calm, restorative retreat in perfect sync with its glorious surroundings.

Terrace furnishings deliver comfort and style to a sophisticated home perched at the ocean's edge. The palette is plucked from the water itself: teal and turquoise of varying shade and pattern drench casual, low-maintenance outdoor fabrics.

A stone coffee table by Michael Taylor delivers durable elegance and ancient Roman flair. Indoors, a modern Lucite coffee table comes alive with an attractive mix of coral and antique and vintage accessories.

The delight is in the details. An old wooden beam from India serves as a valence for an elegant window treatment. An elaborate carving graces an antique chair from China. In a powder room, an ornate vanity from Guadalajara, a richly ornamented floor-to-ceiling mirror, and a gracefully framed antique Peruvian painting are arranged together for maximum impact.

Custom-painted Talavera plates and chargers along with coordinated coral-inspired napkins and rings beautify a dining table. A charming terrace features Moroccan lanterns, an antique industrial cart converted into a table, and an eye-catching view. Behind the pool, a vintage log trough from Thailand is pressed into service as a planter.

My passion for all things Moroccan is on full display in this home. An eclectic collection of unique and spectacular objects, authentic architectural elements, bold color, design motifs, and textured walls melds traditional North African style with contemporary comfort.

Hand-painted dishes from a street vendor in Hanoi and iridescent mother-of-pearl napkin rings from Myanmar set a casually elegant scene on a travertine tabletop. Dining room formality is offset by the playful charm and global glamour of these ornamental accents.

A collection of Spanish pottery displayed on an old Caribbean sugar mold supplements the elegant ambience with the rustic feel of antique earthenware. Living room furniture is arranged on a diagonal axis in order to soften the room's rectilinear design and maximize access to the splendid views enveloping the space.

The organic shape of a coffee table made from reclaimed wood is an effortless way to bring the beauty of nature into a home. A living room environment that celebrates the fusion of old with new, elegant with relaxed, and soft fabrics with hard surfaces also blurs the distinction between inside and out.

A small antique mirror surmounts a painted cabinet in a demure, but gracefully charming, hallway. Facing, the generously sized antique Indian mirror with an intricately carved whitewashed frame makes a major statement in a magnificent foyer. The plain plinth table from Indonesia and simple turned wood play supporting roles.

DOMESTICATING THE EXOTIC

SPRING ROLL WRAPPER
GALETTES DE RIZ
BÁNH TRÁNG

Not everyone is a fellow traveler. Gallivanting around the globe, contacting foreign cultures firsthand, negotiating the confusion of the unfamiliar marketplace and social landscape, soaking up the exotic—these scenes appeal in the abstract, on paper, and in idle daydreaming to virtually all of us. And getting from, say, Santa Barbara to Santiago is way less complicated and overwhelming *now* than it was *then*. But even a quick hop to the Algarve still takes a good amount of planning, effort, time and expense. And disposition. This is my point. The desire for wanderlust or thirst for adventure varies wildly in any group of even very close friends. Not just energy level or Portuguese fluency or disposable income, but a more basic set of personal preferences. While the thought of thrusting myself into another former Soviet Republic appeals to me and many others, it will seem unnecessarily exhausting for those who are happy to meet the world from the proverbial armchair on their home turf, so to speak. That's just how the spectrum plays itself out. Some readers absorb non-fiction accounts of life in gilded, pre-Castro Havana while others prefer to make the journey themselves. There is value in each degree of exposure to the outside.

It's not so important to perform as a worldly jet-setter. If the thought of setting foot on the continent of Africa seems wildly inconvenient, you can quench your thirst for the sounds of the medina, the scents of the souk, and the mesmerizing intricacy of the tiled geometrics by other means. This is where I come in, though it really wasn't even a conscious decision on my part to position myself as an intermediary. I grew toward it for many years, developing a taste for the new and novel and a drive to meet the challenging and the alien head on. Aesthetic curiosity may be what leads me forward and farther afield and to appreciate the indigenous utility and beauty of newly encountered artifacts and artworks, but it is my deep faith in my ability that leads me to search out stories of color and manufacture and motif that grow organically out of distant thriving cultures.

I'm no historian, but my take is no less relevant—there is honor and merit in any marketplace acquisition of textile or carved wood or pottery. Like a relay runner's baton, these transactions represent an exchange of ideas and imagination and tradition from one culture to another. The excitement of discovery is what motivates me to revisit the Egyptian craftsmen of the trouble-

some Middle East whose inter-generational woodworking skills and trial and error of their inlaying process continue to inspire me. I keep returning to the rooftop of the world in the Himalayas to refresh my appreciation for the precious color use of the Bhutanese weaver. The outcome from these happy accidents of my intercontinental meanderings is the privilege of relaying these "batons" to my clients.

In this way, artifacts from exotic destinations are given new life and new purpose in surroundings perhaps continents removed from their making. They may function as aesthetic statements, perhaps sharing pride of place with other veteran pieces of similar journeys. They may also be re-purposed and serve a function completely divorced from the original intention of the craftsmen who created them. Whether I am overseeing the installation of large antique Spanish terracotta olive jars as a focal point in a garden or fountain vignette, or throwing a woven Bhutanese blanket over a table or converting a found piece of carved door into a headboard or tabletop, I am simply relaying a cherished piece of artisanal work with, I hope, a portion of its original context still intact. I might say that I have domesticated these pieces, but that would be a misstate-

ment. To my mind, it is the new owners who have become "exoticized" by their appreciation of these design elements and their willingness to deploy them as aesthetic statements for a conventional lifestyle in North America.

Few may want to comb the Indonesian islands scattered across three thousand miles of the equatorial Pacific for authentic textiles, or sleep in the Moroccan desert like a Bedouin on the hunt for Berber rugs or hitch a ride on an elephant through the Thai jungle in search of a local woodworker. But I do, and I always will be on the search for more compelling and exotic examples. I will always be on the lookout for more imaginative re-imaginations of the dynamic batik textile or neo-traditional usages of teak or sheesham in cabinetry. And these pieces will in all likelihood trade hands again in the secondary markets of their newly adopted homelands, and that is fine too. What is certain is that the world will never cease to amaze with examples of as-yet-unseen solutions or executions in wood or ceramic or glass or silk. And it's also certain that I will yet again take to the airways and highways and byways to seek them out and share the vitality and exquisiteness of these finds with my clients.

A living room space showcases an exquisitely curated collection of vintage, antique, and contemporary global finds. A little Moroccan table, Turkish carpet, and an earthenware pot handcrafted by Indians in Oaxaca merge comfortably with traditional furnishings for a look of effortless refinement. Bright orange pillows on a sofa add a striking kick of color. A pale neutral palette keeps the mood fresh and soothing in a bedroom and living room.

A carved-wood architectural fragment from
Indonesia mounted on an iron stand delivers
a stroke of exotic style to a poolside vignette.
Antique tooled-leather Spanish Colonial
chairs and contemporary patio furniture
work together on a covered terrace that blurs
the distinction between indoors and out.
A candleholder from Guatemala provides
sculptural relief against a chamois-colored wall.

Bold blue stripes on the dining chair backs deliver an assertive counterpoint to the caramel-hued leather seats. Behind the dining table, an antique Indian mirror sourced in Rajasthan leans against a wall. Above, a mother-of-pearl inlaid nightstand from Syria and an antique Spanish trunk at the foot of the bed give this room its international credentials. The blue floral duvet brings delightful pattern to a wooden bed carved in Mexico and upholstered in a saturated goldenrod.

The solution for a 37-foot curving wall that defies the hanging of traditional paintings? I enlisted an artist to create a tropical mural from the hallway all the way around the staircase. In a foyer, a painting on stone by Mexican artist Victor Cauduro Rojas surmounts a 17th-century Spanish trunk and can be illuminated from behind.

Architectural finds catapult this bedroom into triumphant territory. The headboard is fashioned from an old carved door from Thailand. An antique beam from India is transformed into a valence. A Dennis Wentworth Porter painting echoes the green, yellow, and coral color scheme. An 18th-century Spanish trunk and antique Chinese stool round out the vibrant room. Above, a balcony features wicker, a travertine-topped table, and an amazing view. The bedroom is inspired by the natural beauty and Spanish Colonial traditions of the Mexican coastline, which I adore.

Fantastic light, stunning views, and a sophisticated color palette blend with modern furnishings, curving accents, and one-of-a-kind 20th-century sculpture for a clean, contemporary dining room. The custom-designed Mexican star chandelier above the table becomes a riveting focal point.

This room is all about the mix: an Indonesian
entry door converted into a headboard
rubs elbows with a unique vintage wicker
chair, inlaid Moroccan table, textiles, and
artisanal pieces from around the world.

I found these magnificent doors in Alexandria, Egypt, and engaged a local artisan to refinish them. Twisted iron rods with curled finials confer additional handcrafted allure to the scene. The visual effect of a beautiful textile should never be underestimated. Here, a vintage, one-of-a-kind Bhutanese cloth drapes an antique Spanish chair.

The family room, featuring a vaulted ceiling and a wall that opens onto a terrace, is decorated in a neutral palette. Warm pops of color and pattern are provided by a profusion of accent pillows. The stone fireplace unifies the interior and exterior environments, while textural antique vessels enhance an overall scheme of natural finishes.

In a bedroom, an antique French bench reupholstered in cream silk coordinates gracefully with the rug and bedding. This powder room afforded the rare opportunity to conceive design during construction. I had old railway ties installed as shelving and then dropped in a marble lotus flower sink. A carved mirror from India, antique Spanish wall sconces, and everyday Mexican candlesticks finish the look. Although the rich reds and blues in a painting by Mexican artist David Villasenor become the focal point of an entryway, facing, the roomscape also draws upon the colors and patterns of classic Turkish and Persian rugs for the design schemes.

In a bedroom, a headboard made from an antique iron gate stands out against walls treated with a pale yellow wash. The rug is from Michoacán. Two small hallways deliver two striking articulations of old and new furnishings. An old Guatemalan church cabinet houses a Mexican *santo* of the Virgin over a vintage Guatemalan chest. Nineteenth-century altar candles flank an antique Italian gilt box. Contemporary Mexican table, iron sconces, and a recent painting by Dennis Wentworth Porter cheer up this hallway.

Traditional Mexican accents and sophisticated style merge in a visually compelling kitchen. Extremely faux-distressed plaster walls, bright and energetic backsplash tile, and black stone counters bring a sense of excitement to everyday routine. I designed the bar stools out of pieces of reclaimed wood.

A dinner party tablescape pays homage to a recent trip to China, with chopsticks and dragon napkin rings. Hand-beaded place mats and lustrous gold blossom napkin rings create a more formal setting. Vietri dinnerware from Italy is one of my favorite patterns.

An impeccably balanced, beautifully unified interior boasts cosmopolitan flair. International inspirations are Chinese-style lacquered barstools and Venetian-plastered walls. The room's focal point—a Chagall lithograph in a gilded frame—anchors the clean, refined seating area. The bronze hand andirons deliver an unexpected element of surprise. In a chic dining room environment, facing, a Chinese garden stool has been turned upside down and repurposed as a planter for a spray of orchids.

A seashell mirror centers a soft and feminine little girl's room. The custom-
made beds in antique silver and mirrored table provide subtle shimmer
against a wall of soothing seafoam green. Grounded by classic influences like
stripes, a palette of muted teal and cream, and a traditional window treatment
with a valence, the bedroom, facing, exudes a timeless sophistication. An old
Indian trunk, upholstered carved-wood headboard and tropical artwork by
Victor Chavez imbue the room with an exotic spirit.

For this dining room, I channel old-world elegance with my signature modern sensibility. Feminine color and pattern holds its own with the heavy beams, dark woods, and imposing arches. The custom-made *ojo de buey* (eye of the water buffalo) mirror is inspired by an emblematic Mexican architectural motif. The ironwork is my custom design, made in Puebla.

A traditional *boveda* ceiling crowns a dramatic foyer. A 17th-century *santo* stands
on a custom cabinet made in the Spanish Colonial style. The dynamic artwork
depicts a collage of indigenous costumes. Above, Spanish Colonial religious
imagery is evident in this detail of a painted, gilded antique altar cross.

BEAUTIFUL & USEFUL

Tiles, Textiles, and Rugs

I'm no austere minimalist or Spartan modernist; on the contrary, I love more. I just love the right more. A carefully considered acquisition of an enormous, centuries-old Persian Heriz rug is a large investment and also a commitment to ongoing proper care and responsibility. The beauty and utility of these Turkish-Iranian masterpieces with intricate patterning and soft vegetable-dyed hues is worth, to my eye, maybe twice whatever the sticker price might be. Hand-knotted rugs and carpets—whether paisley and Persian, floral and Oriental, or striated and Berber—are basic, elemental. They soften and warm any floor and add dimension and texture, which makes them *fellow travelers* in the best sense of the term. They can be unrolled true to a room's shape or in any asymmetrical manner that appeals. They can be re-rolled and moved and unrolled again and give identity to all subsequent rooms they anchor. Their beauty lasts; the patina of age and use only contributes to their allure, along with exposure to light and perhaps spilled wine and saltwater dripping from sunny hair. I'm sold on them! The bigger the better. They pay dividends for decades.

So do the smaller pieces of textile, weaving, tapestry, drapery, and organic fabrics that I seek out around the world and acquire for clients. Again, textiles have absolute utility as treatments for doors and windows and insulating artifacts adorning walls or even ceilings. They beautifully cast color, texture, and pattern over wooden furnishings and can instantly bring otherwise anonymous surroundings to life.

Textile arts are versatile and can transition from use to use, and that is their true genius. Expertly selected fabrics appear everywhere—on lampshades, valences, table runners, headboards and canopies, cushions and poufs. They may seem disposable by virtue of their size and lack of heft or consequence. But they endure and persist, and there is always room in your next life for Thai silks, Moroccan weavings, printed Irish linens, Peruvian appliqué, and Iranian velvet.

My favorite example of the simultaneity of beautiful-ness and usefulness in the domestic sphere is set tile—whether accented simple pavers or jewel-like intricate mosaics. The tiles themselves can be staggeringly beautiful as individual pieces of art, while the artful setting of tile can deliver overwhelming impact, with unexpected patterns and geometries revealing themselves upon repeated viewings.

That tile is useful is obvious. It has for millennia been a domestic mainstay for use around water and as a passive cooling material, assembled from the simplest and most economical of materials. The three-dimensional quality of tile can impart color to a floor or wall in an entirely dynamic way beyond the reach of any paper, paint or faux finish. It is durable and resilient. And bold. And I like this: a discussion with a client about an installation of tile can sometimes be like a mating dance with some wary tropical creature. Everyone is intrigued by the drama of tile and the promise of bold transformations and exotic transport to some place like the Alhambra or the Hagia Sophia, but there is often trepidation and something like pre-buyer's remorse. I know how floor-to-ceiling tile looks and feels, and I can assuage the lowest hanging fears. The beauty *is* the usefulness and vice versa.

Calm is the order of the day in a dining area whose pale aqua palette reflects my love of the hue. Inspired by the grandeur of Old Mexico, heavy furnishings in the Spanish Colonial style and custom iron fixtures mix easily with bare marble floors and subdued hues. The kitchen beyond is a clean, simple, and spacious presence.

For this guest bedroom, a couple of antique Guatemalan screens are repurposed as headboards. Simple bedding in bright blue is enlivened by vibrant pillows made from vintage textiles—Guatemalan stripes and Mexican florals. Two bedrooms, above and below, demonstrate the visual power and versatility of well-made pillows, which deliver color, texture, pattern, and comfort. They're really the ultimate accessories.

The goal of this expansive living room was to unite the traditional with the contemporary and the exotic with the everyday. The result is a sophisticated, well-traveled aesthetic, at once tropical and cosmopolitan. A Knoll Barcelona chair shares the stage with a six-foot-tall antique Buddha from Indonesia. An English Duresta sofa and old teak coffee table from Bali rest on a cream-colored silk rug from Tibet. Bronze bowls from Vietnam and silver boxes from India contribute to the energetic international spirit of the space.

A spa-like environment pervades this master bath, which opens onto a romantic outdoor terrace with fireplace and hot tub. The luxurious surroundings include marble surfaces, inlaid mosaic design, global accents, and fabulous lighting.

Two small guest bedrooms deliver comfort and style that feels calm and collected. Iron headboards fashioned from old Mexican gates flank an antique Tibetan trunk that serves as a nightstand. Two small Turkish rugs deliver a colorful lift in front of the beds. Similarly, an old Pakistani carved chest separates two beds with upholstered headboards based on traditional Moroccan motifs. Large enough to take on the energy of bold color and lush patterns, this red-and-cream bedroom, right, is feminine without being frilly. The carpet, curtains, and walls in pale neutral tones add calmer shades into the mix.

A fantasy of soft teal tones, this lavishly upholstered bed provides the ultimate feminine retreat. Celadon and citrine silk pillows work with charcoal nudes found in London to add just the right amount of edge and intrigue. Objects of many vintages occupy bedside tables, including Deco lamps and, perched on a stack of books, a tiny pair of antique baby lotus shoes from China, and a Bhutanese bronze Buddhist dagger. Above, a rustic Indian cabinet with hand-painted design looks sophisticated and beautiful in any room. An old Indian daybed is hung from the ceiling of a covered terrace to create the perfect spot for an impromptu siesta.

In this stylish and inviting open living area, plush sofas surround a contemporary Guatemalan coffee table, emphasizing comfort, cohesion, and rustic sophistication. An Indian rug and a framed antique textile carry on the palette of warm tones and complete the look.

A Burmese standing Buddha and 19th-century Chinese export pottery grace
a contemporary Spanish console. The one-of-a-kind chest, above, showcases
the artistry of skilled Syrian craftsmen. Its ornate, eye-catching design is
accented with mother-of-pearl inlay. A Mexican gold leaf mirror found in
San Miguel de Allende is an iconic piece that makes a major statement.
These pieces are becoming harder and harder to source, so I can't resist
buying them when I find them.

Accessorizing is essential to the success of any room. I never ignore the little spaces. Playing with scale, pattern, and color can have a surprising impact on a tabletop or in an overlooked nook that might be otherwise ignored. Carved bone boxes from India, sea shells, and sculptural silver or glass vessels can be surrounded with flowers, candles, or an assortment of fruit to create an eclectic, personal moment.

Stone bowls repurposed as sinks bring neutral color and natural texture to any powder room. Even a lava rock can be converted into a unique basin. Finding the right counter accessories is also part of the fun in creating a beautiful bathroom environment. The mirrors are from Syria and Mexico. Right, an enchanting bedroom space is intimate but delivers high drama. Beds layered with pillows and flowing with drapery create an instant sense of comfort as well as an ethereal ambience. The pale green walls enhance the feeling of an exotic nest.

A vibrant tile pattern energizes the backsplash underneath a custom-carved *cantera* hood in a Spanish-style kitchen. High upholstered chairs surround a marble-topped island. Below, a generous bedroom revolves around multiple views and repeats the rich earth tone palette of the house.

A sunburst mirror ornaments the paneled wall space above an upholstered banquette. In this living room, breaking up the mostly white walls and furnishings with some darker pieces makes the flat-screen TV blend in rather than stand out. The artful arrangement of furniture, lighting, and objects maintains a light and airy feeling for this classic setting.

I love this pretty dining room. The traditional Mexican hacienda-style chairs are upholstered in linen damask and leather. The exquisite shape of an iron chandelier from Guadalajara makes the fixture an instant focal point above, while the woven jute rug imbues subtle texture to the floor below. In a bedroom, above, using bold elements is a great way to manifest a cocoon-like atmosphere. The unique headboard is a pair of Egyptian doors. Contemporary Mexican artwork and Turkish rug flaunt their glorious colors in the room. Italian dinnerware, beaded napkin rings, and a capiz shell place mat provide an exotic departure from the everyday setting.

A headboard made from a Moroccan entry door, nightstands from San Miguel de Allende, and antique Spanish candlestick lamps all come together in a beautiful melting pot of style. Above, Moroccan shutters and an Indian rug dress up this small bathroom with worldly charm. Glamour and drama co-star in a home office designed for a busy executive. The muscular, custom-carved desk is from Guadalajara. Behind it, sepia-toned antique map of the Americas is reproduced on a paneled cabinet and spotlit for arresting effect. The pale sea foam and sand tones in the rug lift and soften the overall impression.

The handsome dark cabinetry almost makes this kitchen feel like a paneled gentleman's library. High beamed ceilings and eggshell-white walls contribute to the sense of openness, while an iron chandelier fits the grand proportions. Green marble counters and cream travertine floors underscore the traditional aesthetic.

IMPORTS & INSPIRATION

Furniture

It's obviously fun for me to wander the northern provinces of India, the jungle towns of Southeast Asia and the souks and *brocantes* ringing the Mediterranean, searching out exquisite textiles and tile fragments and tabletop artifacts. Most of these decor accessories can be acquired and hand-carried home without ever being out of eyesight. Hunting for small treasures is a sport anyone can play—the recreational decorator, the dilettante, the rookie. But the serious big game of the intercontinental safari—the signature armoire, the expansive daybed, the thousand-pound tavern table, the wood, the iron, the stone—are the real trophies of the professional interior designer.

The building blocks of rooms and architecture of living and the backdrop for lifestyle isn't really the fabulous lantern or the pair of stools or the eye-catching gilt mirror. Instead, the real backbone of our residences is the bed frame, seven-foot sofa, table for twelve, china cabinet and banquet-ready sideboard (and architectural relic). It's the big stuff, the big-ticket items; these are the basis for everything else.

I understand the anxiety associated with committing to the large, the bold, the cumbersome, the costly, especially when you happen to chance upon it in, say, Yangon, Lhasa or Kathmandu. The purchase is the easy part, but then the pang of realization: How do I get this antique carved convent door not just back to my hotel but back to the port town of, say, Guayaquil and delicately into some container with duties paid and insurance arranged and dispatched to arrive in Los Angeles months later? Who can be so sure of their taste in a dusty souk? Who can reliably imagine the dimensions and tones and heft of a mosaic table thousands of miles (and sometimes continents) away in a seaside villa, cleaned and repurposed and given pride of place?

I can—no reason to engage in false modesty here. I know these decisions are important and crucial for a client's home and ultimate luxury and satisfaction. Securing and transporting *excellent* pieces is always worth the hassle. I know there are dozens of ways to put to beautiful use a possibly overwhelming chest of the most exquisite mahogany or inlaid bone. The first things out of almost every client's mouth are, "It's too much. It dwarfs everything else we have so carefully arranged. It is too loud . . . " Okay, so guilty as charged. But my contention is that accessories and the good stories that come with them matter not a peso if they are left to swirl around in a self-storage unit. You need room for plates and goblets and serving bowls and lovely linens and candlesticks, and a butler's pantry can't contain all that. Clear the decks and

start with a fantastically rich and heavy new-world Spanish Colonial armament chest or an enormously intricate Chinese glass-fronted cabinet and reverse engineer the entire room.

My thinking is that space is to be revered in any room, indoors or outdoors. And space should only be occupied by something that adds more than it takes away. By this metric, one or even two fantastic carved canopy bed frames from Portugal are entitled to exile any number of banal side tables, lamps and ancillary benches in a bedroom. I'm no "less is more" devotee, but I do say "lose the second string entirely and let your stars perform." I mean, would it kill someone to have to read or eat in bed because that chaise had to go back to the farm? Or share some Rioja or kummel over a refectory table the size of a Bentley, having to sit on top of the thing to get close enough to confess a love of Cartagena *aguardiente* and the aroma of sea air through the gauzy beachside doors?

The truth is that we all need considerable fewer places to sit or eat or store than modern shelter magazines would have us believe. The alternative is to pick a winner as best you can and make the room serve the purpose you need and try not to shoehorn your lifestyle into so many conversation nooks and areas of retreat. I love empty

corners and space to spread out, and if every last inch of wall and floor space is "decorated," there's no room left. With some restraint in the number of furnishings and some exuberance in their size and scope, you may have the best of everything: richly appointed rooms with balance, weight, permanence and story as well as the space in which to repurpose, entertain and improvise.

This is the great contrast and vitality of "tropics thinking," as opposed to the traditional layouts of more temperate climates—great pieces of wood and metal and occasionally glass and stone combined with spacious rooms in which to move them about with the help of some strong men. Like clearing the room for a banquet or festival or dance: roll up the rugs, move the table and live your life. Too much "muchness," tabletop tinsel and extraneous extravagance will put the kibosh on this sort of spontaneous life and festivity. Our rooms are merely backdrops for our own transitory dramas, and who wants to take second billing to a set decorator?

Go big. Go bold. Leave yourself room to breathe. And kick off your heels and bluff your way through that impromptu Paso Doble. Everyone dies, but not everyone *lives*. And, yes, three out of four containers actually arrive at the intended port of disembarkation.

A guest bathroom allows for a unique exploration of color, material, and detail. The custom-carved open cabinet unit accommodates an onyx countertop and backsplash of Talavera tile. For this powder room, facing, I had a rustic antique Afghan cabinet fitted with a bowl from Thailand and repurposed as a vessel sink. The antique French mirror and Ethiopian cross accessory further define the well-traveled character of the home.

An interest in vernacular architecture is the basis for what I do, as well as the ability to mix what is modern with the time-honored. The floor of this wine cellar tasting room is dry stacked with reclaimed old stone, while the curving walls of new stone create a cozy enclosure for conversation. Only the backs of the Portuguese leather chairs are covered in traditional tapestry fabric in order to deliver unexpected nuance. Chandeliers don't just supply light; they also create intimacy, romance, and glamour. On a bed, above, an earth-tone palette unifies a lavish mix of fabrics. An antique Mexican red ware bowl complements the color scheme.

The spectacular view seemed to insist on minimal distraction. I organized a seating arrangement around an octagonal metal Moroccan table and accessorized with pillows fashioned from antique Mexican textiles. Beyond the grouping, an old animal feed trough serves as a planter. The unifying factor—inspired by the expansive open space—is simplicity.

This dramatic living room boasts strong symmetry and exquisite detail. The sinuous lines of the Italianate console and the curved edging of the sofa effortlessly contribute to the overall mood of elegant sophistication. The crowning glory of the room—a magnificent carved fireplace hood—lends the room regal dimension. A casual arrangement of lilies reflects simplicity and nature.

A covered terrace conveys the feeling of outdoor living and continues the palette used throughout the house. My affection for teal blues and greens, which are very soothing colors, extends to a sitting room corner vignette, where a comfortable armchair is flanked by a Moroccan water vessel and a small octagonal side table. I think every great living room should have a dramatic moment, a stellar piece or something unexpected. Here, it's the imposing marble fireplace embellished with geometric contours and carvings. Two 18th-century ottomans and a contemporary Mexican iron coffee table carry on my fondness for mixing the traditional with a touch of the modern.

A cream and teal palette along with a mix of traditional furnishings and eclectic global objects distinguish this crisp, idiosyncratic living area. Walls of untreated windows contribute to the openness and light and convey the outdoor feeling of a coastal home.

In this bedroom, a palette of sunny colors balances out the dark furnishings. Bright persimmon with dollops of moss green and marigold yellow, combined with pale neutral tones of the walls and floor, add to this luxuriously relaxing setting. I believe in surrounding ourselves with the things we love in a beautiful, comfortable, and appropriate way. A client's hand-beaded pillow on the sofa, above, personalizes the space. A framed collection of antique British botanical prints enlivens a hallway.

The most stylish kitchens meld cabinetry and cutting-edge appliances with traditional touches. In this colorful example, I drew on the inspiration of the Mexican culture with inventive tile work and the use of indigenous natural materials, such as travertine and marble. Selecting the right finishes during the construction phase is as important as finding the right furniture. I love having different values in a space, from grand to humble, and using unexpected elements. For this terrace, I started with a rug that looks like sisal but is soft enough to walk barefoot on. Then I anchored the space with an old rustic table that symbolizes the simple beauty found in surrounding farm structures. The unobstructed ocean view really takes care of the rest.

This casual and comfortable bedroom plucks its timeless blue-and-white color combination from the breathtaking view of the ocean. The bedside tables are vintage, hand-painted Indian chests of drawers that go hand in hand with the easy, relaxing vibe.

A fearless mix of color and pattern characterize this dark, dramatic, moody bedroom. An antique trunk from Asia and artwork renderings of cloaked figures lend an almost mystical quality to the room's ambience. For a young person's fun San Miguel de Allende-style bedroom, above, handmade ceramic hearts were used to decorate the walls. A whimsical arrangement of hearts made by a folk artist in San Miguel de Allende animates the bright marigold walls between twin beds. Built-ins are a must! Custom drywall shelves designed for books and personal treasures surround an antique archway repurposed as a headboard. Very old, very rare shells from all over the world are mounted on stands and deliver sculptural interest.

Woven textures, a natural color palette, and imported woodcarvings imbue this warm, inviting bedroom with exotic drama and elegance.

I'm very fond of incorporating traditional religious artifacts in my design work because they capture the spiritual nature of various cultures. Aged objects are handmade and tell stories. This bedroom's antique rustic Virgin is embellished with hundreds of traditional Mexican *milagros*—each ornament representing a prayer sent to God by the person who pinned the small piece of tin or silver to Mary—and artfully describes the soul and style of Mexico.

If we're really honest, it's the spaces between the great rooms—the foyers and the hallways—that give us the experience of moving through a home and make a house dynamic. This hallway is graced with a 17th-century statue of a pope from Italy. Over the centuries, the statue's colors have faded and lost their muscle; peeling paint reveals its simple wooden origins. To restore this Holy Father to glory, I washed a back wall with a golden ochre hue and propped him on a "Madonna" table from an old church.

A powder room becomes dramatic and glamorous with a huge mirror that dominates a wall. A carved console holds a modern black marble sink. Antique gold leaf wall sconces add glimmer and a touch of elegance. In front of an old Thai painting I purchased in Chiang Mai, right, my fabulous French Bulldog, The Bean, looks worried as he sees me packing again. One glimpse of my python travel tote, pashmina, and passport and he knows: Mama's leaving again.

RESOURCES

A RUDIN SHOWROOM
Pacific Design Center
8687 Melrose Avenue, Suite #G172
West Hollywood, CA 90069
www.Arudin.com

AGA JOHN RUGS
Pacific Design Center
8687 Melrose Avenue, Suite #B538
West Hollywood, CA 90069
www.Agajohnrugs.com

ANN SACKS TILES
8935 Beverly Boulevard
Los Angeles, CA 90048
www.Annsacks.com

CACHE
8744 Melrose Avenue
Los Angeles, CA 90069
www.Cachecollection.com

COUNTRY FLOORS TILES
8735 Melrose Avenue
Los Angeles CA 90069
www.Countryfloors.com

DAVID SUTHERLAND SHOWROOM
Pacific Design Center
8687 Melrose Avenue, Suite #B182
West Hollywood, CA 90069
www.Davidsutherlandshowroom.com

DENNIS WENTHWORTH PORTER
Calle Alvaro Obregon, between Morelos and Guerrero
San Jose del Cabo, BCS 23400
Mexico
www.Denniswentworthporter.net

EBANISTA SHOWROOMS
Pacific Design Center
8687 Melrose Ave, Suite #G190
West Hollywood, CA 90069
www.Ebanista.com

ELIZABETH EAKINS RUGS
8550 Melrose Avenue
Los Angeles, CA 90069
www.Elizabetheakins.com

FORTUNY FABRICS
Keith H. McCoy
8710 Melrose Avenue
Los Angeles, CA 90069
www.Fortuny.com

GARY MORELL ANTIQUES
915 North La Cienega Boulevard
Los Angeles, CA 90069
www.Graymorell.com

GIATI SHOWROOM
Pacific Design Center
8687 Melrose Avenue, Suite #B122
West Hollywood, CA 90069
www.Giati.com

JANUS ET CIE
Pacific Design Center
8687 Melrose Avenue, Suite #B146/B193
West Hollywood, CA 90069
www.Janusetcie.com

KNEEDLER FAUCHERE SHOWROOMS
Pacific Design Center
8687 Melrose Avenue, Suite #B600
West Hollywood, CA 90069
www.Kneedlerfauchere.com

KRAVET FABRICS
Pacific Design Center
8687 Melrose Avenue, Suite #B624
West Hollywood, CA 90069
www.Kravet.com

LODI DOWN & FEATHER
6 Empire Boulevard
Moonachie, NJ 07074
www.Lodidownandfeather.com

MARIO URBINA CARPENTRY
San Luis Potosi E/Sonora y Sinaloa
Col. San Jose Viejo
San Jose del Cabo, BCS
Mexico 23437

MATOUK LINENS
Pacific Design Center
8687 Melrose Avenue, Suite #B368
West Hollywood, CA 90069
www.Matouk.com

MICHAEL TAYLOR SHOWROOM
Pacific Design Center
8687 Melrose Avenue, Suite #B542
West Hollywood, CA 90069
www.Michaeltaylordesigns.com

MIMI LONDON SHOWROOMS
Pacific Design Center
8687 Melrose Avenue, Suite #G168
West Hollywood, CA 90069
www.Mimilondon.com

MINASSIAN RUGS
Pacific Design Center
8687 Melrose Ave, Suite #B139
West Hollywood, CA 90069
www.Jhminassian.com

MINTON SPIDELL
8731 Melrose Avenue
West Hollywood, CA 90069
www.Minton-spidell.com

PERENNIALS FABRICS
David Sutherland Showroom
Pacific Design Center
8687 Melrose Avenue, Suite #B182
West Hollywood, CA 90069
www.perennialsfabrics.com

ROBERT ALLEN FABRICS
Pacific Design Center
8687 Melrose Avenue, Suite #B499
West Hollywood, CA 90069
www.Robertallendesign.com

SANDRA ESPINET RUGS FOR AGA JOHN
Pacific Design Center
8687 Melrose Avenue, Suite #B538
West Hollywood, CA 90069
www.Sandraespinet.com

SCHUMACHER FABRICS
Pacific Design Center
8687 Melrose Avenue, Suite #B489
West Hollywood, CA 90069
www.Fschumacher.com

SFERRA LINENS
Pacific Design Center
8687 Melrose Avenue, Suite #B368
West Hollywood, CA 90069
www.Sferra.com

TOMAS ENRIQUEZ IRON
San Jose del Cabo, BCS
Mexico 23400

VIETRI
PO Box 460
Hillsborough, NC 27278
www.Vietri.com

WALKER ZANGER TILES
8750 Melrose Avenue
West Hollywood, CA 90069
www.Walkerzanger.com

ACKNOWLEDGMENTS

The creation of interiors is a team effort and I count on many people to help and support me through it all. I am lucky to count on the following people, who have helped my dreams and this book come true:

Al Kairis—for being the love of my life.

Sabina Todd—for being my best friend

Madge Baird—for believing in me and giving me this opportunity

Mel B—for the introduction and for your great writing

Hector Velazco—for your amazing photography

Debra McQuiston and Melissa Dymock—for a beautiful book design

A special thanks to my tireless staff, whose hard work and long hours make it all happen. I could not do it without them:

Paulina Jimenez—Sr Designer

Queta Guzman—Sr Designer

Caro Castrejon—Jr Designer

Fabiola Flores—Jr Designer

Jeanette Van Wyk—Design Coordinator

Ana Paula Gastum—Interior Architect

Janeth Vidrio—Interior Architect

Malu Santana—Office Manager

Horte Zamudio—Personal Assistant

Rocio Vicario—Installations

Adrian Estrada—Installations

Juan Marquez—Installations

Mauricio Dominguez—Installations

But most of all, this book exist because of the amazing clients who have trusted me through the years with the personal task of designing their home. Thank you all for giving me the opportunity to serve you:

Paul & Penny Loyd

Gary & Karman Parker

Tom & Carrie Corbett

Greg & Vanessa Reyes

Gordy & Dona Craford

Nancy Williams

Greg Reyes Jr.

George &Paula Jauch

Ron & Alexis Fowler

Joe Fryzer

Scott & Suzanne Walker

Ricardo & Martine Weitz

Steve & Debbie Bergstrom

Murray & Gaye Farncombe

Dan & Diane Tsubuchi

Mike & Mary Brown

David & Abby Harbour

Dave & Sharon Merwin

Chuck & Kim Watson

Dan & Diane Tsubuchi

Glen & Teri Morgan

Don & Laura Glatthorn

Don & Leslie Cangelosi

Mark & Deborah Carter

Jim & Gail Norman

John & Leticia Hahn

Joe & Suzanne Sutton

Jeff & Pam Kentner

Text and photographs © 2013 Sandra Espinet
Photographs by Hector Velazco,
except Gray Crawford, pages 18, 64–65, 71, 82–83, 108–09, 124–25, and 128

Published by
Gibbs Smith
P.O. Box 667
Layton, Utah 84041

1.800.835.4993 orders
www.gibbs-smith.com

Designed by Debra McQuiston
Page production by Melissa Dymock

Gibbs Smith books are printed on paper produced from sustainable PEFC-
certified forest/controlled wood source. Learn more at www.pefc.org.
Printed and bound in China

Library of Congress Cataloging-in-Publication Data

Espinet, Sandra.
The well-traveled home / Sandra Espinet. — First Edition.
pages cm
ISBN 978-1-4236-3320-4
1. Espinet, Sandra—Themes, motives. 2. Interior decoration—United
States. I. Title.
NK2004.3.E85A4 2013
747—dc23
2013005930